Searching

{ IN SILENCE }

Vipul Bhesania

Cover Design and Artwork by
Arthur Luke www.arthurluke.co.uk

Searching

{ IN SILENCE }

Vipul Bhesania

to mum and dad -

i will be forever grateful for my time with you in this life.
your lessons will be passed on to those i am
fortunate enough to cross paths with.

and to my brothers -

i am grateful to have a bond with you
that is beyond words.

dear soul searcher,

this is for you.

searching for who i am

searching for why it was me

searching for what pain means

searching for hope

searching for faith

searching for beauty

searching for love

searching for purpose

searching for destiny

searching for meaning

searching for closure

searching for my soul

searching and searching

with no end in sight

because no answer seems right,

so here i am still searching,

searching in silence.

if you're searching too,

maybe we can do it together.

words are a vehicle for emotion.
the words on these pages express the
emotions that have stirred my soul.

i hope they soften the toughest parts of you
so you can live with more love.

these words will find their way to all those
who seek love and guidance.

if you feel like you have no one else,
i will always be by your side in spirit.

the world needs to see the full blossoming
of your beauty before you go.

It won't be the same without you.

it is those who live slightly

      outside the well-defined

     boundaries of society

that will eventually

redefine   them

and show us

what is

          truly possible.

| contents

| foreward

Some write books to make money. Some write to look good. Others write because they must. The latter write from a deeper well.

They write because something dormant has been awakened. They write with a new found awareness, of themselves and the world. They have crossed a threshold where the current of courage flows that little bit more fluently. They write beyond themselves. A place where making a difference becomes more important to them than looking good. They write from the vulnerable parts of themselves in the hope that their writing can help others do the same. They write with the burden of making an impact. They write as if they have to. As if their lives depend on it. Because the parts of their awakened self will die if they don't express their truth into the world.

I met Vipul at an event in Las Vegas where I was speaking. I was standing in line to get a coffee and offered to buy one for a young man behind me. A total stranger who has since become a friend. Vegas must be one of the most disconnected places on earth. A place people go to disconnect from the world they inhabit. Like a good action movie where you can take a short break from your life.

So, how does a young man searching for himself in Vegas write a book of deep vulnerable poetry? I have watched Vipul grow into himself and have been fortunate to play a small role in that journey myself. Vipul attended my BraveSoul experience on Irelands west coast a few years back. The one thing I remember deeply was his smile. It came from his soul. I do not want to attempt to credit my work alone with his transformation, but that smile was different when he arrived. It was dull. It was rehearsed. It was staged. It was expected. It felt heavy.

The only way I can describe the smile at the end of the week was watching someone's face change as the person they love unconditionally walks across a beautiful park towards them. The moment you know its them for sure, and the soul bypasses the mind and overflows with the sheer unpolluted love you have for their beautiful soul. It looks like the deepest form of acceptance. It's the smile that can only emerge when you have forgiven the person for their flaws, and accepted the ones that won't go away. It's the kind of smile you see a mother give their newly born child. It's the smile that emerges from the most compassionate part of you. That well of compassion that you often starve yourself of.

The person that Vipul met that week, was himself.

His poetry will not introduce you to him, his philosophy, his mission or his beliefs.

His poetry will allow you to meet yourself.

Philip McKernan. - Author & Healer

who am i? }

i slowly peeled back the layers of who i thought i was
and there waiting for me was, my original self.
the one that was always there and will always be.

beautiful, unmarked and pure.

this human costume comes with lots of potential attachments
and that makes it hard to live on earth sometimes,
i found myself dissolved into the costume and I became
acquainted with the costume and forgot about the wearer.

i write this to open a portal between

the costume

and

the rest of the cosmos,

to open communication with the cosmos so that
i can ascend further into my journey and finally find out
why i was chosen to be here,

to be right here,

right now.

who am I?
i am just me.

who is "me"?
who said the word "me"?
my inner voice.

where is the inner voice coming from?
nowhere.

what does "nowhere" mean?
not any place.

silence.

the truth was whispered eons ago,
those who are quiet enough,
will hear its echo.

i am not my name,
i am not my body,
i am not my job title,
i am not any title,
i am not my salary,
i am not my ambition,
i am not my dreams,
i am not my ethnicity,
i am not my race,
I am not my religion,
i am not my personality,
i am not my experiences,
i am not my memories,
i am not my opinions,
i am not my thoughts, either.

i am not who you think i am,
i am not what my parents say i am,
i am not what my brother says i am,
i am not what my teacher says i am,
i am not what the media says i am,
i am not what books say i am,
i am not what my friends say i am,
i am not what society says i am,
i am not what i say i am either.

all of those things are an external description of me,

but   I   am

so   much   more.

to find me you must remove all of your masks,
the ones you wear to stay safe,
to stay hidden,
to fit in.

aren't you tired of wearing them all the time?

take them off until you find there is no mask left to take off,
until you've finally found your real face again
and you'll know when you find it.

It is the faceless one,
swimming in love,
drenched in passion,
and continually expanding.

It is the one that will remain
long after all your other faces
crumble into the earth.

my body is only a scarf warmly
wrapping my soul for a short while.

when i disconnect from my senses,
my torso,
my organs,
my head and
my thoughts,

what is left?

a never-ending silence.

that is what i am.

silence is the foundation for all other noise.

whenever there is too much noise going on around you,
take a moment to listen to that silence within,

it's

your

eternal

resting

place.

but who is "me"?
who is the one speaking?
who is the one listening?
who is the one thinking?
whose thoughts are these?
who am i?

i am no one,
i am no thing,
i let go of all disguises and realise, i am everything.
I am all possibilities.
I am the known
and the unknown
wrapped in magic and mystery.

we are all like trees with roots deep inside the universe,
connected in mysterious ways,
waiting to cross paths with "the one",
while we try to figure it all out,
asking similar questions,
looking for love,
searching for meaning,
and searching for purpose,
without realising we all live under the same roof
(look outside and look up).

we've all felt intimidated,
confused,
disappointed,
and lonely.

we all cry,
laugh,
smile,
and stress.

we're all human,
we're all here,
i'm writing,
you're reading,

it's one big adventure
that we're all on together.

listen to your heart beat,

it is the echo of the entire universe.

what if we could remember what it was like being inside the womb?
the warm comfortable feeling of floating in pure water,
being held with a deep knowing that everything is ok.

at that point,
do we know who our mother is?
do we know we're inside?
does it matter?
do we feel the split between ourselves and our mother?

i don't think we do.

we feel as though we are one.

there is no sense of boundary -
this seems to happen after birth,
when we develop our ego.

It's the protection mechanism we build to create our place in the world.

if we removed all boundaries the ego created, what are we?

we are one.

one with what?

one with everything that has a pulse on this planet
and all the planets beyond this one.

so then,

where does the boundary of "home" really begin and end?

the human experience is funny,
let me tell you why.

the costume we wear,
the mask we wear and
the personality we create,
is all a brilliant disguise for our true identity.
and we go about most of our lives
based on this deceitful disguise.

If we dissected ourselves,
dived beneath the skin,
under the organs and
beyond the blood,
we'd find we're just a bunch of stuff neatly
held together by a thin coloured sheet.

so then,
what really makes us, us?

It's that deep feeling of connection inside our heart
connecting us to everything and everyone equally.

if we all lived and loved from that place,
what we could do individually,
never mind collectively,
would be truly magical.

because that feeling knows no limit.

it is not in space,
it is not in time,
it is not destructible,

it is love manifesting itself in all the ways it can in this dimension.

where do we go when we sleep?
who are we without our memories?
what makes our heart beat?
what is the force that is breathing us?
what makes us blink without us thinking about it?
who is it that hears me when i speak?
what is doing the walking when i walk?
who would we be if we healed our trauma?
how would the world live if everyone was kind?
what if everyone had their heart open?
what if people saw pain as part of their journey to finding happiness?
what if we learnt from children instead of conditioning them?
what would children teach us if we let them teach?
what if we weren't limited by our five senses, what would we experience?
what if we didn't live in fear?

i wonder.

daily experience seems void

without passionate presence.

nature uses a language that isn't words.

let go of trying to understand everything
through your current knowledge.

in fact,
let go of everything you know,
and suddenly you will know it all.

you'll feel a gradual climax of love
for the infinite potential inside you as it blossoms.

if you notice this blossoming,
you can share it with others.

if you don't,
that's ok,
you'll still die beautiful,

just in secret.

the boy sat quietly on his bed one evening
and reflected on the concept of god.

it seemed everyone thought of god as a man
sitting in a room upstairs in the sky watching over us
at all times from birth to death,
and then we either go to meet him or
we go to meet his enemy, the devil,
but the boy felt this idea was rather odd,
If there was a man in the sky why could no one see him?
and why is he called "him" and not "her"?

then a thought entered his heart;

what if god wasn't a person after all,
but an experience inside each of us?

a great feeling of joy gushed into his veins
as he tasted a glimpse of who he really was.

let the present moment carry you away.

when you're riding the wave of the universe,
it will gracefully carry you from moment to moment
and you won't remember walking there.

the earth will support you,
the wind will guide you,
the fire will keep you warm,
the water will nourish you.

It is one continuous experience.
there is no beginning and no end.
it's all just here,
in the place of vast emptiness of existence itself.
language is weak in the face of experience,
your tongue will dissolve when your heart is awake.

we're hiding under an umbrella.
behind sunglasses
and inside a coat.

we so desperately want to stay comfortable that
we disconnect ourselves from nature and forget
what it feels like to be one with our surroundings.

once in a while,
walk in the rain without an umbrella,
stand in the sun without sunglasses and a hat.
go out in a t-shirt and let yourself feel the cold.

let the earth energise you,
and see what happens.

a grain of sand is no less important than the shore,
a wave is no less important than the ocean,
a ray of sunshine is no less important than the sun,
a petal is no less important than the flower,
a toe is no less important than the foot,
you are no less important than everyone else,

we're all one big organism.
one interconnected family,
interdependent and interrelated,
even if you can't see it,
what you do to yourself,
you do to everything else.

if you pause for just a moment,
you'll hear everyone's heart beating together.

our ego is the series of attachments we've made
in the physical world to help shape our identity.

don't be too distracted by them.

your true nature is not any of these things.

you   are   the   space

between   the   words,

not   the   words   themselves.

don't forget to study the most important subject,

your self.

knowledge comes from outside of you,
wisdom comes from within you.

wisdom cannot be taught,
she can only be tasted when
the boundaries of the ego begin to dissolve.

allow your soul to melt into the universal soul,
and reconcile that long-lost feeling of wholeness and fulfilment
and know that you belong to something beyond just your body.

   - message from miss anima mundi

you don't have to know who you are,

you'll find out who you are.

that's what this journey is for, remember?

what are children but eggs
that have hatched
from the womb of
another grown child?

parents claim their child
as a prize they have won and
name it, clothe it and teach it
to become what they see as 'correct'.

a child is the universe manifesting
itself through yet another costume,
expressing itself in a way that
wasn't previously possible,

until now.

every atom in this world was moved in perfect harmony
to birth this beautiful child so it could express itself
in its unique and authentic way.

but parents want to hold on to them like a prized possession,
a polished trophy that sits quietly shining inside their cabinet.

who dares detach from their child?
to let them live without the interruption of their own ego?

who dares to let their child run free in the wild
with no expectations?

who dares to let their child walk across borders
and swim past boundaries?

who dares to let their child experience something
that has never been experienced before?

who dares to allow their child to ask questions
that have never been asked before?

who dares not name their child
and just lets them be?

who dares to call their child successful
simply because they are alive?

i dare you.

as he was walking,
the boy heard the sound
of an autumn leaf crunch under his foot.
it was a sign of the end and
the sign of a new beginning,
he noticed how the leaf had fallen away,
but the tree always remained.

he wondered if his body was just like the leaf,
eventually withering when it was time to leave
and something underneath would remain.

when we are born,
we are given a name not chosen by us,
we wear clothes not chosen by us,
we go to a school not chosen by us,
we are given a religion not chosen by us,
we are told what is right and what is wrong,
we are delivered into a world not created by us.

who are we when we strip away the labels, beliefs and desires
fed to us from our first breath?

who are we when we forget all the knowledge we were taught
and tap into the wisdom preinstalled within us?

who are we when we remove all the boxes
we were given to place everything?

who are we with no box?

it seems to me,
without a box,
we are free

or maybe freedom is just another box.

the level of separation in our generation
is devastating and frustrating
everywhere we turn,
and everywhere we look,
there lays another form of manipulation,
the content and the platforms we consume,
devoid of any inspiration,
i hope for a better future
one in which we all come together
regardless of our differences and preferences,
uniting because we can
and willingly reach out to
hold one another's hand
living life together,
and nurturing our land.

the biggest downfall of humanity is the illusion of separation.

we are all one stream of consciousness,
experiencing ourselves in unique ways
as we coexist in this malleable realm we call our world.

remove the veil of your limited beliefs
that have come through your five limited human senses
and you will see
that you and me
are no different than
him or her,
a tree or flower,
snake or bug,
soil or sand.

we just chose different costumes for the party this time.

unzip yourself to reveal your self so
you can brighten the darkest places
of the world with your true beauty.

did you ever notice
the universe
has a million faces,
yet,
she remains faceless?

i am a stranger,
and so are you.
everyone is a stranger really.
we don't really know them.
our parents, brothers, sisters and friends.
they are all strangers here to have an adventure.
they have lived so many mysterious lives before this one.
they carry so many adventures, burdens, wounds, magic and beauty
that we will not understand.

so, when they do something upsetting,
let us remember they have things from many lives
that they are resolving and learning from.

it's their journey and you have yours.
It's ok to be on separate pages in the same book.

you are two strangers,
who have met on a train for a short while until you reach your destination,
then it is time to walk away and join some new passengers
on a new train,
going to a new place.

i am channel for divine intelligence.

my only job then, is to be the best channel I can be
and I do that by removing all the things that could
block the divine signal from swimming into my soul.

note to self:
the things i need to unblock will continue to change as i change.
i must listen every time my soul knocks on the door of my heart
to let go of something. and that won't always be easy to do but
it will make space for new experiences to come through.

who are you when you are not on stage?

the secret is in between the words you speak,

inside those brief moments of silence

that seem to hold nothing,

but actually,

carry everything.

if you told the stories of all the lives you have lived,
it would fill all the libraries in the world.

i know you like to travel the world,
but have you seen all the beautiful places inside of you?

be a tourist inside of yourself for a day
and you will see the most beautiful sights.

if you don't see them before you die,
you have died blind my friend.

as you walk further down your path,
you'll need to change your clothes a few times,
because you'll grow out of your old ones or
they might become raggedy and torn from
all the battles you've faced,
and that means some people will no longer
recognise you in your new outfit.

that's ok,

because you're not the same person who first set off on this journey,
and you'll meet some new people at the new place you're going to.

look in the mirror,
do you see that long line of people behind you?
they are all your ancestors who were waiting for you to arrive,
they all placed their bets on you,
and now you're here,
they're watching you play the game,
while they protect you along the way,
so don't be scared,
you are a million bodies wrapped into one,
and their protection is stronger than any body armour you can buy.

discovering our true selves is the only adventure
all of us are really on.

from birth to birth as we incarnate
with different masks each time, we ask;

who am i this time?

why am i here and what is it i *really* want?

we peel back the layers of who we think we are -
who society has told us we are,
and find out who we came here to be.
then we need the courage to be that.

through this journey we will fall in and out of love with ourselves,
we will fall in and out of love with others
and fall in and out of love with the work we do.

but the most important thing above all,
is that we feel love at all.

once upon a time,
my perfect friday night was drinking until
my heart opened on the dance floor,
and now,
there isn't such thing as "perfect" or "friday"
these are labels we made up
but i'll tell you what,
i'd much rather sit with a hot cup of tea
next to a warm heater,
listening to instrumentals,
and write about my heart,
while i stare at the night sky
wondering if someone knew that one day,
i'd be doing just that.

the stars look upon us every night and wonder,
maybe tonight is the night they will understand,
that when they look at us,
they are not looking at the sky,
they are looking in the mirror.

there was a time when popularity seemed
to be the answer to all my questions,

but now I've realised,
by spending time alone,
I had the answers all along.

i was the magician,
the trick
and
the audience,
all in one.

In our dreams,
we visit another reality,
one that doesn't exist here,
and doesn't make sense to us,
it seems like nonsense when we reflect on the dream,
because it's the place where the
wildest, most unimaginable possibilities, actually happen.

but what if,

it wasn't just a "dream"?

what if,

we travelled to another dimension?

what if,

we are all multidimensional beings
that time travel and space travel every night?

what if,

we're inside that dream right now?

each one of us is
a solution to another's problem,
an angel for another's devil,
medicine for another's pain.
we are all pieces of a cosmic puzzle,
but we can only see the picture if we
allow ourselves to come together in unity.

though I live here,
i am the citizen of no country,
i am the resident of no town,
i only live inside your heart,
that is my only true address,
the eternal address,
you can find me there, always.

why do I feel undercover in my own life?

living a double life,

Infiltrating people on earth,

nowhere to call home,

trying to find a safe space

but nowhere seems to be the right place

my own body doesn't seem like home

I'm trying to pull this mask off my face

doesn't work though,

seems like I'm stuck with this race,

but who am i?

and where is home?

what i am doing here?

remind me,

what's the cure for amnesia again?

with every negative thought I create
with every negative word I speak,
with every negative action I do,
i am a killer.

with every positive thought I create,
with every positive word I speak,
with every positive action I do,
i am a creator.

some people walk a long pilgrimage to find me,
and still they do not realise
i am secretly walking
by their side the whole way,
hoping that one day they know
i am not only at the end of their journey,
but I am at the beginning and the middle,

i am always there.

i am the soul who quietly writes words
that will one day change the world
to be a more whole place once again,
the way I remember it all those lives ago.

it is one song expressing itself
through many instruments,
you are one of them,
let your version of the song be heard.
because someone out there is waiting to dance.

he looked up at the sky and in frustration said,
"where are you? i can't see you anywhere!"

a gentle voice responded,

"looking for me is like looking for your eyes,
but when you look in the mirror.
you see your eyes,
think of the world as your mirror,
i am not in one place,
i am in every place,
all the time,
walking,
running,
and sleeping
right by your side"

sometimes it feels like
i'm looking at the world through a window
i can see what's going on
but I don't feel involved in any of it,
it's as if my body is from this place,
but my soul calls home to another land.

somewhere
between
childhood
and
adulthood,

we seem to lose ourselves.

we have been born into structures made before our arrival,
but we have the choice to stop constructing them
and create plans for a new world,

one

where

we

choose

what

will

define

us.

recognise that some ideas have
gone past their expiration date.

leaving behind a rancid smell
but let us not forget,
it was someone before us
who came and casted that spell.

now it's up to us to be courageous enough
to replace the old and give birth to something new,
something we can tell our children we helped create
and give them a chance to see the light,
before it's too late.

maybe,

it is not what we do that defines us,

but by how much of ourselves we have   d I s c o v e r e d.

we are one cosmic body
with multiple branches,
wherever we go,
we are visitors nor guests,
we are home,
just with a different view each time.

service,
silence
and
serenity.

those are the nicknames i want.

my skin is gently holding together
hundreds of bones and lots of organs,
but if i was sliced open
and all my bones and organs fell out
i'd be an empty costume that was brilliantly held together by a lie,
my soul is nowhere to be seen.
did it escape upon opening?
or was it never really inside to begin with and
was plugged in from another place far, far away?

me?

i'm not really anyone

and,

I'm everyone,

all
at
the
same
time.

we are all connected
beyond our face, race and faith,
beyond our gender and level of slender.
why is it so difficult to see then that when we are hurt,
we bleed the same?

the mirror is a funny place,
it plays tricks on you,
it's a tool from the devil to confuse you,
every time i look into it,
i only see the ugliest parts of me,
the costume I came here with for free,
it keeps the beautiful parts hidden away,
kindness, compassion and courage
are strangers in the mirror,
yet we look into it for hours judging ourselves,
the mirror is a funny place to be,
because it only tells half your story, you see.

i see now i was born asleep.

i began following the signs
and slowly began to awaken.

there seemed to be a reality beyond this one -
beyond the one my senses were showing me.

it is though i have been placed inside a painting
and the urge to tear the sky filled my soul,
the wonder and awe of what lay beyond captured my heart
like nothing i had ever felt before,
it was a fire of burning desire to know,
to not know knowledge,
but to know truth.

to know the truth
we were born into,
but too blind to see,
too numb to feel,
too deaf to hear.

trauma }

when i dropped the lens of seeing people through titles,
i realised everyone was just a human with a story,
wandering souls trying to understand life.

and from that place,
i could connect with them all.

there are emotions we have suppressed,
that are attached to a memory we don't want to remember,
quietly sweeping it under the rug hoping it won't resurface,
but to remember it and accept it, will dissolve its weight.

emotions are energy in motion,
if they are trapped,
it is as if a plastic bag has been forced over our soul,
and we become sick.

let's not keep them in a cage,

let them   b r e a t h e

so we can feel free once again.

sometimes our wounds are there to show us

who we really are underneath

all

that

skin.

**your trauma can be your teaching If you're aware
of the lessons it has to teach you,**

then you have the gift of teaching others
and liberating them from suffering too.

lift the veil of anxiety, confusion and hate from your eyes,
and you'll see the world in a whole new colour.

you don't always need sunshine to grow,
the darkness is growing you in the places the sun can't get to yet
let the darkness hug you for a while,
because when the sun eventually rises again,
it will meet fertile ground and
help you blossom in a way you couldn't before.

we all have a story,
but only some of us are courageous enough
to read it,
<u>accept it</u> and
share it with the world.

many of us walk around with insecurities
that we don't want anyone to know,
but by stepping into them you
automatically free yourself and
attain power and peace that you
couldn't have otherwise received.

by putting yourself in that vulnerable place,
you allow others to feel safe enough to share
so they can feel liberated of the weight they are secretly carrying.

free people of their insecurities
by stepping into the insecurity yourself.

if someone has been in the dark for so long,
they'll be blinded by the light.
so be gentle and be kind.
they have to build their way back to your love.

everyone acts from their level of trauma.

if someone is lashing out or acting negatively remember,
they have faced something in their lives which has
made them insecure and unstable in that very moment.

those who are jealous, angry, outraged and frustrated
are those who are most lost in life and
are longing to remember what it feels to be loved.

joy suppressed will manifest as anger.

the cure?

laughter.

with each smile,
each giggle,
and each roaring laugh,
joy will crawl its way out of suppression
and dissolve your burden into bliss.

let it all go.

the heaviness in your heart, let it go.

the chaos in your mind, let it go.

the pain in your body, let it go.

notice your clenched fist, let it go.

smile, because you can.

before the hate,
before the anger,
before the fear,

you were just pure love and wonder,
but you've forgotten that,

let your guard down and open your heart again.

it's worth it,

you're worth it.

my face was taken from me,
I was left helpless, lost and unarmed,
I was caught off guard,
It was at that time I felt alarmed,
because I knew I was in for a hard battle,
who do I run to for help?
all directions seemed like a dead end
I went to the doctors - the ones i thought I was safe with,
the same ones who prescribed drugs to destroy me,
and fooled my body into healing symptoms but leaving the root,
sleepless nights consumed me,
laying like a corpse as my body deteriorated,
I tasted torture and smelt like death,
maybe I should use my "get out of jail" card and remove this pain,
because i'd had enough of playing this game,

but,
i didn't let it consume me,
for a minute I let you fool me,
but you weren't going to take me,
not this time,
because deep down I knew I had more to do,
though it felt like the end,
i put the card back in my pocket
and I see now that in fact,
It was just the beginning.

one day the boy realised,
it didn't matter what his external appearance looked like,
he now saw the sun, moon and stars in the mirror,
and when he looked outside,
he no longer saw the sun, moon and stars,
he saw himself.

and on the same day,
there was a girl millions of miles away
who wrote this about herself,

"the faith in her heart moved mountains,
she became unstoppable when she
finally realised she was the only one
who had to believe she was worth it"

forgiveness will break the cycle.

forgiveness will free you.

forgiveness will empower you.

forgiveness will heal you.

forgiveness will complete you.

forgiveness is the secret to closure.

let go of the old,

and the new will knock on your door.

(they can't be in the same house together)

self-judgment comes from comparison.

if you don't compare,
you're less likely to judge.

and if you don't judge,
you're free to be who you are.

the heart is where the secrets of the universe are.

the heart is our connection to others.

the heart is our connection to divine intelligence.

but we have locked our hearts away and thrown away the key

take a breath and let your guard down,

let your love flow once again.

unzip the suit you're wearing,
take off your mask and be free.
don't be ashamed of who you truly are,

shame is a learned behaviour.

when we were born,
we weren't comparing ourselves to others,
we were simply happy because we were happy,
there was no reason needed.
It was our natural state of being.

but we grew up and began comparing ourselves,
and the feeling of insignificance crept in.

ignore it.

you were born beautiful and you will die beautiful,
everything in-between is just a thought.

think about it.

when we begin to heal ourselves,
we become a channel for healing others.

if you begin by saving yourself,
you'll begin saving the world.

note to self;
healing begins with one simple realisation-

you did the best you could with
the knowledge you had at the time.

we all want to be seen and heard,
it makes us feel like we matter.

trauma arises because we feel like
we haven't been respected or appreciated in some way.
so, anger, jealously, hatred and frustration
find the back alley into our mind,
and close the highways to our heart.

by ignoring what is broken,
it doesn't magically make it fixed.

maybe it is time to hug your demons
so they can finally melt away and
clear the road to your heart.

because even demons have feelings

don't jeopardise other people's chances of feeling love
because of what you've been through,
the best gift we can give one another,
is to commit to love each other more deeply.

and unfortunately,
for that to happen,
you must see past your own hatred
towards yourself and the rest of the world.

everyone has an opinion about us
based on the lens they're looking at life through.
once we learn to accept ourselves,
we won't need acceptance from anyone else.
self-acceptance is our superpower,
it is our medicine,
It is the gateway to relief,
relief that we no longer have to hide and fight
to become someone we're not.

we are too drunk on our wounds
and too sober in love.

it is during our darkest hour
that our brightest self is born.

during the dark hour we say goodbye
to who we once thought we were
but we tremble, not realising it is indeed a blessing.

the next version of you will now appear,
the version that can handle the blessings
that have been put in a basket with your name on it.

remember,

the same outfit isn't always appropriate for every occasion.

the sad girl was alone in her room one rainy evening,
and while staring into the mirror she felt a pang of
sadness in the pit of her belly because she felt
she didn't like herself very much,
as the tears began rolling down her face,
she heard a voice say,

"my dear child I wish you could see,
that you are nothing less than perfect,
because I don't ever make mistakes"

we protect our heart so it doesn't shatter,
because we know it is the most valuable thing we have,
but a wise woman once said,

"courage, is living with your heart wide open"

no judgement,

no expectation,

no pressure,

put simply,

accept and allow.

each of us are rediscovering ourselves in our own way,

fighting our own battles and

seeking answers to our own questions.

so when we meet one another

let's remember to mix a drop of

compassion and kindness into our interaction.

please be aware:

> every time you get angry at someone,
> It is burning your body on its way out of your mouth
> before it reaches and scars them.

it started raining and the boy had forgotten his umbrella.

he was just about to run into the shelter
when he remembered what
the old woman had told him in his dream;

"the truth is hidden in the sun and hidden in the rain,
you must be able to find it in both to really understand"

and with that,
he continued to walk facing his palms out
feeling the fresh drops of water as they gently landed on his hand.

it was right then he smiled and thought,
without the rain the flowers couldn't grow,
maybe everything had a reason for happening after all.

he began to suspect his "burdens" were part of a much grander plan.

she felt the devil was always on her back,
but she couldn't yet see her path was different,
the devil was teaching her how to carry more weight
so when the time came,
she could lift the heavy hearts
of all those that needed support.

to be broken into a million pieces
means you now have a chance
to put the pieces back together
in whatever way you want.

i was scratching my skin like a scratch card,
the open wounds provided space for new light to enter,
the blood poured out impurities
and made way for the pure,
i was turning to ashes
and being born again.
ascending through time
a little bit stronger
and a little bit wiser.

when my self-worth gets tired
and decides to take a nap,
self-judgment peeks its head from under the duvet,
and worthlessness jumps on the bed to join in
and I begin feeling like i'm not enough
i compare myself to others and sulk for a while
seasoning my wounds with salt
by looking at a snapshot of others
and dreaming of the perfect photo album they must all have.

one day she realised
she didn't need the light
to see in the dark,
she needed to change
the eyes she was using,
from the ones on her face,
to the one inside her head.

life can be dark sometimes
but those are the moments
the light is preparing itself to shine again.
It's just like how the night becomes very dark
when the sun is preparing to shine again in the morning.

frustration said,
"why is he angry all the time?!"

anger shouted;
"because everyone is always doing things to annoy him!"

self-hate joined in;
"he doesn't like himself very much and
it comes out on all those he loves the most"

then a quiet voice from the corner of the room spoke,
it was compassion, she said,

"adults are just grown children with a buried past,
let's invite curiosity into the room for a conversation –
it's been a while".

curiosity gently came in and said;

"the past can be like a box that you live out of,
it is part of the reason you are who you are today,
you have a story because of your past,
but, it does not need to limit you,
it can only limit you if you allow it to dictate
your reactions toward current situations,
change your reactions and maybe, just maybe,
the current situation will begin to change a little".

i'm a cloud holding everyone else's tears,
no wonder i feel heavy at times,
i forget to let it go
so i can feel light and fluffy again.

recognising your weakness

is a sign of strength.

_ν_

the most devastating conviction we've inherited is

the distance between us and god.

nothing lasts forever,
the light,
the dark,
the sunshine and the rainbow
they all have to leave
because even they are only visitors
in this cosmic hotel.

if i could time travel,
i'd visit all the people in the world
right before they were about to kill themselves
so I could give them a hug and tell them
everything will be ok.
what would the world look like if they were still alive?
but since i can't time travel,
I hope these words reach you
before you make the decision
to leave forever,
before your time,
because I want you to know,
that darkness doesn't last,
just hold on a little longer,
because sunshine told me
she's coming for you next and that
some of the happiest people
have had the saddest lives.

how many people are on the edge right now
one step away from death?
quietly hoping for one more person to care
just one more soul
to give them hope that things can be better
and then maybe
instead of taking a step forward,
they'll take a step back
and avoid death for one more day.

staying alive takes more courage than dying,

so, if you're reading this,

well done you courageous human.

underneath the skin
we remain the same
our scars and our sins
remind us we're not the only ones
insecure and insane.

after all is said and done,
maybe the definition of happiness
is being ok with just the way i am.

the thing I want to know is,
how do I bring the peace I feel while I sleep,
to the life I live whilst i'm awake?

sometimes a long hot shower

is all the therapy you need.

maybe if you wait another day or two
the feeling will pass
and your heart won't feel so black and blue
but that requires faith
that everything happens for a reason
and that this is only a season.

i want to feel magical again
but darkness,
she seems to follow me,
and suffocates my heart
and I'm left wondering
if this moment was written in my birth chart.

when you're in the thick of an emotional situation
and hope seems to play hide and seek,
he's hiding because he's teaching you
to be stronger,
to believe in yourself
and to become self-reliant.
the darkness is a time to transform into
the new version of yourself.

ps – god said she turns the lights off
so nobody can see you while you change.

i feel like throwing my brain on the floor and;

d i s s e c t i n g
it

so I can find the part where self-hatred lives,

                              because i really need to remove him,
before he starts spreading
and influencing other neighbourhoods
where the sun still shines.

sometimes it feels harder to smile than it does to cry.

where's the address for happiness?
i want to meet her
and ask why she hasn't visited yet
have you seen the map to her house?
then please let me know,
because there's a long line of people waiting to go,
all I want is two minutes of your time
to ask you why you're so hard to find
there's so many of us searching for you,
many claim to have seen a version of you,
but none of them hit home for me
i'm beginning to think maybe happiness isn't your real name,
and if that's the truth then it's a shame,
because that means we've all been searching
for something that doesn't really exist.

simply holding space and listening to someone
will help them more than your words will.

compassionate silence is a pillow for the wounds,
a place for them to rest and heal.

I like believing tomorrow could be better than today,

and that it's all happening for a reason,

because even if it's not true,

it's comforting to imagine

the sky can be a little more blue.

and then one day she realised

inner peace was more important than
all the other goals she had set herself.
it was the one thing that would help her
in every area of life
for the rest of her life.

many years ago,
when she was just a child,
she felt disturbed, distressed and disregarded,
and when she grew up to be an adult,
she had neatly tucked away those feelings under her heart,
but if she wasn't careful,
and didn't heal those wounds,
she would continue to mistake sugar for salt the rest of her life
and push away all those who really care about her.

dear sad human,

I know it feels like no one can hear you
and no one will care,
and you're questioning yourself -
like why is this happening to me it isn't fair,
but the trees sway violently in the wind this evening,
they feel you're about to cut out a root from the ground
by taking your own life,
they're warning you to stop and think twice,
It isn't easy to face this stormy weather alone,
If you're reading this,
it isn't your time to leave yet,
this place on earth is still your home,
so please don't leave so soon,
don't make your exit just yet
because there's so many beautiful souls
waiting for you to connect.

numbness,
it's not a nice place to be,
i've been there and sometimes still dip in and out of that place,
it's scary because when you can't feel,
you don't feel human,
you don't feel normal,
you so badly want to reconnect with your inner self,
but you can't feel it anywhere.
you want to cry - but you can't.
you want to laugh - but you can't.
you want to smile - but you can't.
your heart is beating,
but your body isn't animating.

what I've realised though is,
numbness means the universe has given you an anaesthetic.
It's performing surgery on you and protects you from the pain
while it secretly builds your character through all of the rain.

everyone sees the calmness on my face,
no one sees the chaos in my heart,
I guess it's because they feel miles and miles apart,
my head   and   my heart.

dear suicide,

you're calling my name,
persuading me to leave the game,
not feeling emotions anymore seems so sweet,
but to end it all means giving up on my gifts
and to never know how many lives my life uplifts,
If I listen to you and leave now so many will be left helpless
I can't be selfish,
not yet,
I have to stay strong and soldier on,
It is hard - but I'm not going to follow you
because i can feel it's not the end yet,
though it feels like an apocalypse within me,
i can't believe i've come to a place where
I'm face to face with you and
one simple decision stands between

everything

and

nothing.

but like I said, not this time,
i'm going to turn around and walk away
i won't be persuaded by you now,
not today.
flirting with you has made me realise life and death
are both only one breath away.

repeat as many times as you need to;

i am being healed

i am being guided

i am exactly where I need to be right now

love }

the parts you find most scared to share about yourself,

are the ones i want to love.

when self-worth comes from self-love,

you'll never feel worthless, ever.

like seeds,

we are packed full of potential,

self-care is the nourishment we need to fully blossom.

and that means watering your garden first

so you can share the fruit with everyone later.

fill yourself up with so much self-love

that it spills over into others.

creating boundaries to protect your energy
is a form of self-love.

it's not selfish.

I only have so much energy on a daily basis.
It is important to use it towards my development
and not my destruction.

i wonder if meeting my soulmate,
will feel like the smell of fresh lime.
- a new beginning.

we try so desperately
to fill the void within ourselves
with love from another
and that creates the chaos of co-dependency.
but if we fill the void with our own love,
the love of another creates passionate coexistence
and then their love,
well,
it's a bonus.

bond to empower one another,
don't try to fix yourself through her,
because if you try to build your relationship with half-love
and try to make her live up to your expectations,
eventually your heart will grow rotten,
and the smell will distance her from you.

and then one day he thought,
if he couldn't even love himself,
how would he ever love anyone else?

he felt the empty space
between who he was and
who he thought he should be,
and it couldn't be filled with anything
apart from his own love.

he had some more work to do,
he wasn't ready for her yet,
because if she came along today
he wouldn't know what to say.

even those who hate
are showing love
in the best way they know how.

the sun competes with the light you shine on the world every day.

she carried the light of a thousand suns
rising at the same time,
the warmth of her hugs melted away his
anger, anxiety and anguish.

every time I cry,
another dam is broken within me
that was previously blocking my heart,

the more I cry
the more streams of love
seem to flow through me.

I cry not because I'm sad,
I cry because every ocean in the world
is pouring through me.
I am overwhelmed with love
and each tear has the entire ocean inside it.

life begins the day your heart is open.

love ripens the heart,
spread it more,
and quietly increase the dose each time,
people will eventually become sweeter,
because love gently pushes
the walls of the heart to expand.

can you guess how many people had to fall in love for you to be born?

love brought you to this very moment.

i imagined what her ecstasy felt like

long before I met her.

that evening when they embraced each other for the first time,
an ineffable current ran between them both,
they knew they were meant for each other
like two pieces in a jigsaw perfectly fitting together,
when their souls merged and became one,
their minds dissolved,
they were entirely immersed in the moment
the feeling of passion drenched each of them in bliss,
suddenly the illusion of separateness fell away
and the merging of two energies took place,
it became a playful experience of diving deeper
and deeper
into the merging.
their ecstasy ceased to be individual and
it became one simultaneous experience
mutually exchanging energy
in a perfectly synchronistic way,
and right then,
in that very moment,
they had tapped into the heart of the universe
as it began continuously expanding within them both,
they were living and dying in every moment.

when you become connected to a place deeper within yourself,
you realise there is more to you than just your external appearance.
it is your unique energetic signature.
the energy and presence you carry with you
in every interaction you have with another being
others can feel yours and you can feel theirs.
as you become more acquainted with this energy,
you realise everyone is connected,
because we all come from the same source,
and we carry it in a variety of ways.
when we connect to this energy,
we seek to find energy in others
that will balance the energy within us,
it is like a natural gentle pull toward a certain aura,
the beauty we seek then comes from a place underneath
the costumes we wear and not from the costume itself.

when he was quiet enough, his soul said,

"don't forget to feed me too.
your body needs food,
I need love
and not just from others,
but from you"

the one person you find hardest to love,
has been divinely placed there
to teach you how to love unconditionally.

even though it was winter,
when she smiled,
it felt like summer
and the sun seemed
to shine a little brighter.

love comes and goes
because one of you grows,
and that's ok,
maybe it's time to dance to another song now.

when she was born,
the earth stopped spinning just for a second
because she had taken its breath away,
and the earth whispered to the rest of the galaxy;

"she's here, the one we said would teach
the world to smile again, she's finally here".

and in that moment,
the whole universe stood still
because it knew
nothing would ever be the same again.

when I looked at her,
i saw a thousand stars shining,
she carried the light of the moon in her eyes,
and the warmth of the sun in her heart.

the depth of her beauty
caused ripples in my soul,
and suddenly I knew,
this wasn't really the first time we'd met,
we were about to start a new chapter
of a book we decided to write long ago.

instead of fighting all the parts of you that are abnormal,
cherish them and show them off,
because no one else has these rare gifts,
and if they are rare,
you get to choose the price.

i thought fairy tales weren't real,
but then I met her,
and the world turned animated,
and seemed a little brighter,
my heart began pouring honey,
my eyes softened into pillows
gently catching her warm gaze,
my lips trembled,
and I suddenly realised,
i was holding a real-life picasso painting,
it was the one that hadn't been sold at an auction yet,
because no price was good enough for her,
the only payment she would accept was
someone with an open heart and open ears,
and no one had given that to her, yet.

those we are closest to in this life
are the ones we began the journey with
long before we were born.

dig deep enough and
you'll find we all want the same thing.

connection.
community.
appreciation.
acknowledgment.
love.

on repeat.

some mistake my tears for sadness,

but it's the rain from the sky
that has nowhere to go that day.

sometimes love tastes bitter,
and if you could see the full blueprint,
you'd understand your pain is grace.

- mother ayahuasca

if we all did something kind for someone
and they passed on the favour,
eventually,
the whole world would be a domino of smiles.

the best conversations are the ones
that go on for hours after the sun has set
when the city has fallen asleep
and its just the both of you
unravelling the mysteries of life together.

by honouring my body,
i honour the divine,
because she has chosen to live within me,
would i pollute the home where she lives?
let me not pollute my body with that which does not
create a higher vibration,
negative energy and thoughts must only be
fleeting visitors and not tenants,
self-love is not selfish,
it is a sign of respect to the divine.

it was a love beyond anything he could imagine,
something that made time stop in its tracks,
because even time couldn't keep ticking
when it saw the way she loved,
her love felt eternal, divine,
with no beginning and no end,
it was oxygen to his baby heart.
it went beyond the senses,
it was the kind that made his hearts' heart full,
a feeling no other woman could give,
it had a purity that pierced life's truth,
it crossed the barriers of the physical,
into the mystical,
and back again,
It was the eternal hammock his heart rested in,
to lullaby his every cry,
with each hug. she recharged his spirit,
with every meal, she nourished his soul.
she was the woman god used as a cloak to hide in,
and lucky for him,
she was his mother this time.

when it rains,
it is our ancestors' tears,
for they cannot stand to see us
leaving our homes with hate
and forgetting love on the windowsill

as he looked into her eyes,
and drew her close,
they were both in awe of the ecstasy they felt,
when their lips met for the first time,
it was as if two planets had collided,
then love peeked its head from around the corner,
and with a cheeky smile watched as the boy and girl
blended into each other without a care in the world,

if your identity is centred around
being loved and appreciated by others,
you will never really come to know yourself.
because from this place we only understand ourselves
through love, affection and appreciation others give us.
we are outsourcing our worthiness.

but,

if we begin to realise our own self-worth,
we naturally fill ourselves with love and
begin to find self-confidence,
our love will radiate outward and attract
the right people and experiences who need it most.

when I asked him what his secret to success was,
he shared three things;

1. show relentless love to people (to be noticed in a busy world means the world).

2. sharing love will open unexpected doors for you.

3. put service above money.

in an ocean of sadness,

a smile can create waves of joy.

he knew he was down to his final few breaths,
so he placed her hand over his heart and said,

"i promise to find you again on the other side,
so we can do this all over again"

and with that said,

his breath became air.

there are two forms of detachment.

you can choose to leave with bitterness
and keep your energy stained with hate forever

or

you can choose to leave with love
and let your energy continue to flower forever.

bitterness is seductive,
but flowers smell better.

as he sat with his eyes closed in the sun,

he thought about the girl of his dreams,

the one he could feel,

but not yet see,

the sun began to shine brighter as it giggled,

because from where it was sitting,

it could see the girl he was thinking about.

I am sending love to you
in all the places
it hasn't reached yet

her single smile
was powerful enough
to turn a thousand frowns
upside down.

after one too many conversations with the devil

a thought occurred to me,

what if he was just an angel with a broken heart?

an angry angel,

searching for love in disguise

so, I asked him,

and of course,

he denied it

but that made me smile,

because denial

was the first step towards acceptance.

sad girl,
I don't know your situation but
whatever it is,
It was given to you because you can handle it
just know you are not defined by any comment section,
you're unbroken and beautiful inside
i hope one day
you see what I see
when I look at you
a shining star full of love and potential.

she had just the right amount of twinkle in her eye,
that's how I knew.
I wasn't looking at just another girl,
the twinkle was a sign from god
that this time,
i'd been sent a star.

lead with love,

even if they choose not to.

the words I long for are the ones that don't come,
the one that do not arrive at my tongue,
maybe they do not need to arrive,
maybe this moment doesn't require words,
maybe words will ruin the moment.
by putting the feelings into the tiny curves and crevices of letters
they are limited in their expression.
maybe the most beautiful moments don't require words,
maybe they require me to be ok just being there in silence
and not trying to speak when my breath is being taken away.

L et

O m

V ibrate

E verywhere

what really makes a home, a home?

not the amount of possessions or
the amount of people that live there,
nor the country or the city in which it is built,
nor how big or how small it is,

but the amount of love that lives inside each room.

purpose }

your purpose is to create whatever arises within you,
it is the universe gently nudging you to help it

e   x   p   a   n   d

sometimes I just feel lost,
like a little boy,
who lost his mum at the supermarket.

when all the decisions she made with her eyes open failed,
she began living with her eyes closed,
and then the magic really started.

but none of this is by accident,
many years ago,
in a secret cave somewhere in the corner of the earth,
a wiseman wrote in hieroglyphs
that someday a boy will walk this earth
and will use words to heal people.

maybe he wrote something about you too.

your purpose will change as you evolve,

it is fluid

and changes with who you're becoming.

when it is time, it is time,
no sooner or no later
will the plan be revealed to you.

trust in the magic of it all a little more.

each event in life is like a star,
it seems randomly positioned.

until one day,

you step back and realise,

a galaxy was being built for you.

if you force a flower to open before it is ready,
you will destroy it.
It takes time to develop and grow,
don't be in such a hurry.
a baby takes nine months in the womb,
If it arrives too early there will be complications.
you're being ripened for your mission.

- written by patience

let the strings of your heart play
to the metronome of the universe.
if you follow its cue,
you will never miss a beat,
and you'll create a perfect symphony.

we have come for a brief moment to
sip from the fountain of infinity.
those who have found the fountain
are able to help those who are thirsty.

don't try to become someone,
you as you are, are enough.

you are existence unfolding and expressing itself,
if you want to give yourself a fancy title whilst you're here -
knock yourself out,

but remember,
you won't take any titles with you,

the only thing we leave behind
is how we made people feel,
the energy we created
and then gave away.

your purpose begins as a search for love within yourself
and as you get closer to uncovering more of it,
your intuition will turn the dial on your purpose
and you'll feel it is to give away
all the love you've found within yourself.

I know one day I will die.
but if I die in service to others
then I won't really be dead.
my love and my energy
will have found refuge in another.
and in that way,
I continue to live through the light of love.

what if your purpose was to be angel for
someone who needed saving in this lifetime?

maybe this time you don't need saving,
you've been saved many times before.

have you ever wondered what your role in someone else's life might be?

you may be an angel for them -
the saving grace they've been waiting for.

so don't give up yet because that person will need you.

she said,
"serve people"

i asked,
"why?"

she said,
"well, what else is there?"

experiment without expectation

and soon you will stumble across your gift.

your energy is your real signature
and you sign off on the world
when you leave this incarnation.
don't focus so much on the "what"
but focus on the intention with
which you want to do something.
do everything with love and be of service,
all else will be taken care of.

    - your future self

relax and let me take over, she said.

be still and let me settle.
be still and let me connect.
be still and let me love.
be still and let me flow.
be still and let me be.

don't talk, listen
don't listen, feel
don't feel, be

be ok being still,
it's where clarity comes from.
you can't see the bottom of the pool
unless the water is still.

i often look outside and wonder,
where are we?

what are we supposed to do here?
how did we get so lost online,
that we forgot how to live life offline?
why do we do things that bring a smile to our face,
but a frown to our soul?

my divine purpose and the blazing passion in my soul
is brilliantly covered by billboards, posters and popups.

yet the voice in my heart says;
there must be more to life than collecting materials and titles?"

and my soul replied,

"i am not here for me,
i am here for the collective ME,
the work i must do is to better serve and
help the seed of divinity blossom in others"

chase meaning not money.

do the things that tickle your heart
because the roaring sound of its laughter
will be echoed across the galaxies.

we've come here for answers to questions we think are important.
but in reality,
we've come here to find a part of ourselves
that we don't understand yet,
to find the part we lost along the way,
the one that we hope will make us feel whole once again,
to close the gap in our fractured heart,
we arrive full of expectation and
soon realise emptiness is what we seek.

though you're feeling broken

you're not alone,

you're here to find your gifts

and give them to the world,

to help light the way for those who feel they have no other way

the ones who are frightened without a voice

and afraid to express what they really want to say,

i know it feels hard to hold on,

but just do it for one more day,

and then another,

and eventually you will see

your pain will help lead you to your gifts

because wounds are often an opening to your gift

so hold on

and soldier on

your life is a platform for service

and you're here to raise more lives than you've lived,

so please don't take your life

before you realise what it's for.

i know every day feels like a chore,

but i promise you with all my heart,

on the other side of this, there's more.

you've been passed the torch
so you can light the way for others,
don't let it burn out before you realise what it's for.

In the end,
your joy will come from
what you have created,
not what you collected.

sometimes it's good to be in the dark
because you can't see,
and when you can't see,
you're free to imagine.

dear darkness,

when you first made an appearance

It was just a small shadow,

little did I know this time you were going to grow

to give me a full cleaning

from the inside out and the outside in,

I wouldn't be the same again from within,

I panicked because you took away my vision,

the one I planned every step of my life with using precision

you took away my identity and took away my soul,

I was left feeling helpless and stuck in a hole

but now I see you were teaching me

to evolve and to grow,

dear darkness,

thank you for your lessons,

now I understand your job is to prepare

for the sunshine to rise in the morning.

don't plan the journey,
walk the path that lays before you
and let it surprise you,
isn't the adventure more fun when
you don't know what's coming next?

you may always feel out of place.
not every experience,
every person,
every interaction,
every preference,
every desire,
is meant for you.
you might be feeling like you're on your own.
that's because you're not here to fit in
but to find your place as a guide.
and the people that need guidance will
will find their way to you.

as your path unfolds,
material possessions and
social status become less relevant,
connection to your heart and
to your fellow humans will become more important.
possessions don't have feelings and memories, people do.
what are we really here to do
if not to connect more deeply
with one another and lend a helping hand?

the truth is,
we all want to live free,
but only some of us
are brave enough to remove
the shackles of delusion,
to live the life
we were born to.

as the sun begins to rise,
it is slowly devoured
by the darkness of the night,
the night lulls it to sleep
so it can rest for another day,
because even something as
powerful as the sun needs to rest,

don't be so hard on yourself,
take time to rest in between
your pursuit of meaning.

there is a time to work and exert energy
and there is a time to receive the result of your effort.

don't be so busy doing that you forget
to slow down and receive the miracles
that might be knocking because
you're too busy to open the door.

have the courage to slow down to receive the magic.

oh, and just a reminder before you turn the page;

this is the time to trust yourself fully,
trust your own answers.
it is no longer the time to rely on others to guide you.
where you're able to go on your own will be magical.
say yes to your Self this time.

the sun rises each day
as a sign of hope
that better days are coming.

you are walking on a divine map,
wherever you go,
whatever you do,
it's all part of the plan.
trust it.

when my heart speaks,
it provides no logic,
so i immediately know the answer,
but have no explanation.
magic, i guess.

they say the price of anything is the amount of life you exchange for it,
i've spent 28 years trying to look for this thing called purpose,
you might have heard of it.
23 years of formal education and i still feel a deep sense of separation,
between what I know
and
what I don't,
rowing and rowing and rowing across the ocean of life
and I'm stranded.

everyone's given me their map to find the way,
but it leads nowhere,
then I start thinking; am I even from here?
this planet seems foreign to me and to be honest,
it's boring for me.
sometimes i talk to the plants
and the trees
and maybe even the breeze,
and they seem to give me more answers
than the people with degrees.

oh please, both you and i know a degree doesn't mean you're smart.
everyone has one
and those that do seem to be full of knowledge,
but have no wisdom,
so how can I trust them?
i'm not looking to learn more,
I'm looking to live more
and everyone around me seems to be bad at it.
It's like I'm living around professional actors
who run from rehearsal to rehearsal,
when did life become hurdle after hurdle?

who's got the answers then?
who do I turn to?
maybe i'm taking this whole thing too seriously
and I just need to learn to smile.
but I just can't seem to shake this feeling,
it's like answering this question is part of my healing.

everyone seems to know what they want to do
and I'm still waiting for an email from god
giving me instructions on my next step.

one day I feel like I'm on the right path

then the very next day

I wake up in the middle of nowhere.

some days this whole thing seems like an illusion
and every day i'm flooded
with more and more confusion.

the problem with the "follow your dreams" advice
is that you have to actually know what your dream is.
and that answer never came easy to me
until one day I realised
all I craved was a life full of
depth and purpose.
maybe that's the dream I should chase.

"help me find the sunshine in the rain", he said.

i always wondered
what the point of imagination was
if we didn't use it?

lessons mother taught me:

1. "serve in silence" - do things for people without the attachment of recognition or acknowledgment.

2. surrender to the flow of life, you are not in control, the universe works in mysterious and magical ways. you don't have to know how the magic works to enjoy the show.

3. open people's heart so they can see the world through love again.

4. your body is a vehicle for consciousness, respect it.

5. holding space for others is a gift and a form of healing for them.

6. patience – season your life with more of it.

7. where you are right now is right where you are meant to be.

8. you are being guided, always.

9. your sole soul purpose is service.

10. do not judge yourself or compare yourself to others. you are ok just as you are.

11. you were brought here by grace. grace is the invisible hand that carries you through life. trust her. you're sitting on her palm right now.

12. humility – realise you know nothing and everything, all at the same time.

where is time?

which clock is it we are following?
different countries have different times,
isn't that odd?
the only time I follow is divine timing.

Isn't it funny how you get closer
to a goal,

                                        then it moves again,

and

you

never

seem to

reach   the finish line.

what if my only job
was to believe in the magic of others?

everyone needs someone to believe in them
maybe i can be that someone for you.

the secret to life, my dear,
Is finding magic in the mundane
and then the mundane
won't seem so boring anymore.

i'm not writing for anyone's attention,
i could care less about that,
i'm writing to remind myself
that this is part of my ascension,
to remember i'm here is to be connected again
with everything and everyone
to love and to serve
to heal and to help
to create harmony and not hate
and when all is said and done
I hope i've sealed a beautiful fate.

the love within me was growing so tirelessly,
and it had nowhere to go but on paper,
the words ran out of the pen
as if they had just found their calling,
and i enjoyed watching it unfold with every word.

there comes a time when
answers from books, courses
and other people
don't satisfy you anymore.
it's a sign of your soul growing.
it is telling you to begin
trusting your own answers.

i felt something flowering within me
and i was drawn to water it.
i have become the gardener of the galaxy within me,
carefully and lovingly attending to the soil of my soul.
i know not which seeds have been planted there
but i feel they are thirsty and i'm excited to see them blossom.

death }

don't rush so much,
where are you going so fast?
the finish line is death.

death is the birth into another life,

another adventure,

another experience,

the end of one adventure and

the beginning of another.

or just a milestone in a never-ending adventure.

your expiration is the birthday for your next adventure.

when you take your last breath in this form,

something somewhere around the world

is taking its very first breath,

and just like that the circle of life continues

into a flowing dance of divine unfoldment.

when you leave,
the stars will cry,
the moon will howl,
the sun will hide behind the clouds.
and a few more autumn leaves
will float gently to the ground with grief.
but then,
you'll return once more,
and earth and her friends will quietly rejoice
and warmly welcome you back.

there is no death.

life is a series of births until you reach ultimate liberation
and become one with source energy.

to die a little every day,
is to make room for more
fresh life to grow within you.

remove the business and find the stillness,
there you will realise there is no birth or death,
there are only checkpoints from one world into another,
just like a game,
when you finish one level the character doesn't die,
it is merely placed in a new environment,
wearing new clothing,
with a new mission.
their purpose for that new level may have changed,
but it's still the same person who began the game.

as i sat back and took a deep breath under the sun,
i realised we were all patients in a cosmic hospice,
every being i'd ever met was on their way out,
some sooner than others, but they were all going.

death wasn't an event, it's was a process,
and the process began the day we were born.

so in a way,
right in this very moment,
we're all dying together.

every being holds a vibration on this earth that is unique to it.
once it has vibrated the world enough this time around,
it is time for it to leave.
Then a new vibration is born to
continue its work in a new way.
the whole game is not random,
but a divinely intelligent plan of building the universe.
we are here to build a house of love.
and we do it in a different way each time we incarnate.

if you could take yourself high enough into the sky,
you will see that death is just a birth elsewhere.
the universe is never left unbalanced.

when one heart stops beating,
another begins.

the spirit takes refuge in a new heartbeat to lead another life.

i won't let you say goodbye so

make the most of every interaction.

- death

he could feel it in his heart,
the time had come for him to leave the body.

he asked, "where will I be going next?".

she replied, "where?"

he said, "isn't there a place after death that I will go to? where is that?".

with a gentle smile she said, "there is no 'place' you will go to. you'll become a source of hope for the next truth seeker on their journey. come i'll show you"

he closed his eyes and sunk further into his bed.

a few minutes later in Indonesia, a couple had received the news they were pregnant after 14 years of trying.

we die every night in sleep
to be born again in the morning,
we died on the first night of our arrival
and every night since then.
do we fear going to sleep?
when we are sleeping,
we are nowhere.
our logical mind is not present and yet,
we do not doubt we were sleeping
and will soon awaken once again,
so why then do we really fear dying?
It's the same as sleep,
but instead of waking up in the bed we slept in,
we wake up with a new life.

when i die nothing will be mine,

the moment I was born

I began walking toward death,

and everything i pick up along the way

is a temporary fix

to help me cope along the way.

none of it is really mine,

it's all on loan until my time to leave,

everything I attach myself to is just helping me get from point A to point B.

I mustn't get too caught up in the day to day happenings,

and allow myself to be weighed down by the past or the future.

because the only thing that matters,

Is be right here right now

and feeling the lightness of my being.

don't be afraid,
when you close your eyes for the final time
and open your eyes,
you'll be awake in a whole new world.

when we move from the material space
to the spiritual space,
we have to let go.
the material is a dense place with lots of energy,
but spirit, she's a pond of lightness,
with no weight and no limit,
and to get to her,
we have to let go of unnecessary weight,
so let it all go,
because she is calling you to come closer each day.

if you could see beyond what your eyes can see,

you will see that everyone who has died is still here.

when your breath stops,
It has finally found freedom
to explore the depths of the universe,
but just for a brief moment,
because soon it will find solitude
inside another being who is ready to
take its breath for the first time again.

you have dropped so many bodies to get to this one,
so don't be afraid to drop yet another,
this isn't your first rehearsal,
soon it will be time to change into another costume again
for a new adventure.

and guess what?
She will be choosing your costume for you,
and i hear She has great taste,
so I'm sure you'll look beautiful.

we all die,
but only some of us
choose to live our truth,
the rest die with their truth
in their pockets,
maybe they'll share with us next time.

a villager was once asked why
he seemed so happy with so little
he smiled and said,

"because I do not own anything,
everything I have is borrowed for a short while,
Including my life".

too many die
with untold stories
and unlived dreams
that could inspire
a new world to be born.

the little boy took a deep breath and told himself
this time i'm going to do it,
so he closed his eyes for a moment,
then knocked on death's door,
when she answered, he asked,
"why are people so scared of you?"
she smiled then knelt down next to him and replied,

"I don't know, all I really do is babysit
until it's time for your next adventure".

when I die,
you can bury me or burn me
but only,

if   you

can   find me.

hand me the body bag
It's that time again,
the new me is clawing
his way through,
itching to be free,
ready to be born
and to bury the old me.

every now and again the time will come
to shed your skin.
the painful process of letting go of
what you once knew to be true about
all your beliefs and your desires.
during that period,
you may feel the universe
is demanding a lot from you
and that it's unfair.
but,
it's your soul's growing pains.
you're about to become
stronger, wiser and more faithful than you've ever been,
if you heed the call and allow the universe to do its thing.
hang in there a little longer and you'll see.

the funny thing about death is,

it never seems to come at a convenient time.

until next time soul searcher,

thank you for taking the time to read.

if any of these words sparked something within you,
it is because the words shone a light
on something
that was already there
deep inside you
waiting to be discovered.

if you have read this far to get to the end of this collection of writing,
it is because you are part of a family of beings here to help heal humanity
in your own way.

you are searching for your identity, love, trauma, purpose, death and
exploring existential questions because deep down you know there is an
untapped and unexplored depth to understand and to remember.

if there is only one thing you remember, please let it be this;

**by healing yourself you are healing the world - to fix your own
vibrational alignment is to fix that of the world's and the only control
you have, is over your own vibration.**

if you can find your way back to your true self you will be healed.
as a result, you will begin positively healing others around you.

you are here to do bigger things than you think,
but it begins with healing and finding yourself.

| acknowledgements

to Philip McKernan,

thank you for all the work you are doing to help heal all those who need it. you pushed me to be courageous enough to see my wounds and open up so I could fully accept myself. you will always be remembered as the catalyst for my healing journey. I cannot express enough gratitude for the role you have played in my life. thank you for reminding me that our greatest gifts lie right next to our deepest wounds.

to Tracey Ivanyshyn,

thank you for showing me what unconditional love feels like. you are a light for so many in this life. I love you dearly.

to my closest friends,

thank you for being supportive and present throughout the crucial moments of my life to help me heal and provide a safe space for me to grow without judgment. without your love and laughter, the journey wouldn't be as fun as it has been.

to Jonas Ketterle,

thank you for providing the world with the gift of ceremonial cacao. your cacao served as medicine for me to reconnect with my heart when I needed it most.

to Parker Sherry,

thank you for your guidance as my soul was preparing to cross the bridge between planes of consciousness and heal. i am deeply grateful to have met you along my journey and because of you i will always remain grounded by these words; para el bien de todos.

to Katie Nguyen,

thank you for believing in my words long before they were published and for seeing a vision for me that was bigger than i imagined for myself.

to Vex King,

thank you for bringing inspiration and healing to the world through your words. you are more than just a friend; an older brother and guide giving me heartfelt hope, support and advice when i need it. you lead by example and have remained grounded in your truth in the face of change. you embody self-love, compassion, kindness and humility. thank you for being your true self and showing up each day.

to all the giants i now stand on the shoulders of,

thank you for helping to inspire creativity within me. I want to specifically mention Rumi, Hafiz, Kabir, Khalil Gibran and Paramahansa Yogananda. thank you for opening my eyes to a world beyond this one. thank you for being courageous enough to express the depth of the emotion you experienced during your lives. your words cut through the body and reach the soul.

to divine energy,

i call you "universe" but you go by many names. thank you for weaving together this beautiful and magical journey.

Made in the USA
Monee, IL
17 May 2021